J
811.54
Flo

Florian, Douglas

Summersaults

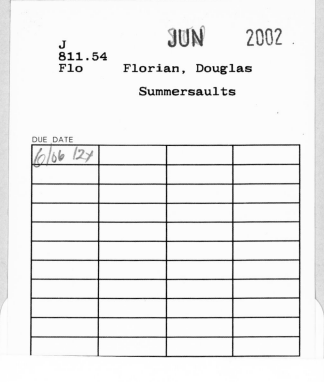

DUE DATE			
6/06 12/			

Summersaults

Poems & Paintings by Douglas Florian

Greenwillow Books
An Imprint of HarperCollinsPublishers

Summersaults: Poems and Paintings
Copyright © 2002 by Douglas Florian
All rights reserved.
Printed in Hong Kong by South China Printing Company (1988) Ltd.
www.harperchildrens.com

Watercolor paints and colored pencils were used for the full-color art.
The text type is Schneidler.

Library of Congress Cataloging-in-Publication Data
Florian, Douglas.
Summersaults: poems and paintings / by Douglas Florian.
p.   cm.
"Greenwillow Books."
ISBN 0-06-029267-9 (trade). ISBN 0-06-029268-7 (lib. bdg.)
1. Summer—Juvenile poetry. 2. Children's poetry, American.
[1. Summer—Poetry. 2. American poetry.] I. Title.
PS3556.L589 S86 2002   811'.54—dc21   2001023619

1 2 3 4 5 6 7 8 9 10
First Edition

FOR ISRAEL LALLOUZ

Contents

SUMMERSAULTS

<pre>
                    l
              u   t
           a   i
Summer is a v   n
                        g thing.
It summer-saults its way past spring.
Turns cartwheels,
      backflips,
Has a ball
Until it t
        u
          m
           b
            l
             e
              s into fall.
</pre>

What i love
about summer

Morning glories
Campfire stories
Picking cherries
And blueberries
Riding bikes
Mountain hikes
Bird calls
Curve balls
Short sleeves
Green leaves
Swimming holes
Fishing poles
Nature walks
Corn stalks
Skipping stones
Ice cream cones
Double plays
And barefoot days.

What I hate about summer

Skinned knees
Ninety degrees
Long droughts
Blackouts
Dog days
Summer haze
Bee swarms
Thunderstorms
Humid nights
Mosquito bites
Clothes that stick—
I hate that summer goes so quick.

DANDELION

The dande-lion doesn't roar.
It's quiet as a closet door.
Nor does the dande-lion race.
All day it stays in just one place,
Except for when its seeds are flying—
Believe me,
I'm not dande-lying.

GREENAGER

Green grass.
Green trees.
Grasshoppers
With green knees.
Green frogs.
Green toads.
Green snakes
On green roads.
Neon green
Tennis balls.
Summer's green
Wall to wall.

THE SWING

The swing's a flinging zinging chair,
The place to chase the air up there.
Just hold on tight, no need to steer,
And soon you'll clear the atmosphere.

The summer trees

The winter trees are sparse and spare.
You barely see a bird up there.
But after the spring equinox
There's flocks
        and flocks
               and flocks
                   and flocks.

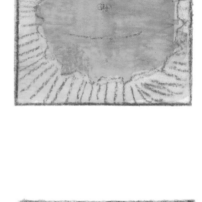

SOME SUMMERS

Some summers *blaze.*
Some summers *haze.*
Some summers *simmer.*
Some summers *shimmer.*
Some summers *sizzle.*
Some summers *fizzle.*
Some summers *flame.*
No two summers
Are the same.

DOG DAY

It's hot and it's hazy.
My body feels lazy.
My clothing is clinging.
No songbird is singing.
The temperature's torrid.
My temperament's horrid.
Has anyone thrown
This dog day a bone?

BEES

I'm pleased by bees
Except for one thing:
The sting.

No fly zone

Fruit flies.
Fireflies.
Damselflies.
Deer.
Dragonflies.
Fairy flies
Buzz my ear.
Horseflies.
Houseflies.
It's getting hotter.
Somebody get me
A six-foot swatter.

DOUBLE DUTCH GIRLS

Double

        Double

Dutch girls

        Double

Double

        Dutch.

Our feet

        are fleet

To catch

        the beat.

The street

        we barely

Touch.

        We never

Trip.

        We're hip,

We skip.

        All day

We love

        to play.

We are

        the best.

We'll never

        rest

Until

        our hair

Is gray.

GRAZE DAYS

On sunny days
We cows all graze.
For days we graze on grass.
And all we've seen
Is grass so green,
Green grass as hours pass.
We chew and chew
The grass that grew,
Green grass from day till night.
And wonder why
That by and by
Our milk is always white.

SIDEWALK SQUAWK

The sidewalk isn't just for walking.
It's good for talking
And for chalking,
Also running
While you're sunning.
I like biking,
Sidewalk hiking.
Cool for scooting,
Roller-skating,
And for super-celebrating!

Names of clouds

Rain maker.
Sky shaker.
Street flooder.
Earth mudder.
Monsooner.
Picnic ruiner.
Mr. Twister.
Mrs. Mister.
Soggy fogger.
Waterlogger.
Blue blocker.
Sun mocker.
Hurricaner.
Plan detainer.

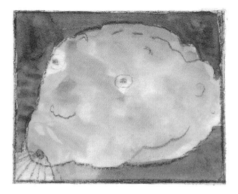

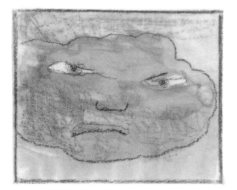

THE SUM OF SUMMER

The sum of summer
Is one billion bees
And six trillion leaves
On three billion trees
And four fillion flies
And five sillion fleas
And uncounted numbers
Of sweet memories.

Summerize

June's a bright blue butterfly.
July is brighter yet.
August is a purple one.
September is the net.

OTTER BOY

I'm not a boy.
I am an otter:
A streamlined torpedo
That speeds through the water.
With grace
I race
Across the pool,
An otter boy—
Until there's school.

LOST AND FOUND

Along the shore
I found six shells:
Two gray,
One white,
Three caramel.
I also found
Nine shiny stones,
Ten pennies and
Four sharp fish bones,
Five feathers from
A seabird's wings.
I wonder: Who
Has lost these things?

THE SEA

Footprint eraser.
Shorebird chaser.
Sand replacer.
Earth embracer.

Tennis menace

We hoped for football,
               baseball,
                    soccer,
But now our hopes
Sit in a locker.
The rain detained
Our plans for fun.
Table tennis, anyone?

Fly ball

He said he lost the ball in the sun.
That game we lost instead of won.
No trophy now,
Not even a plaque.
And the sun won't give that lost ball back.

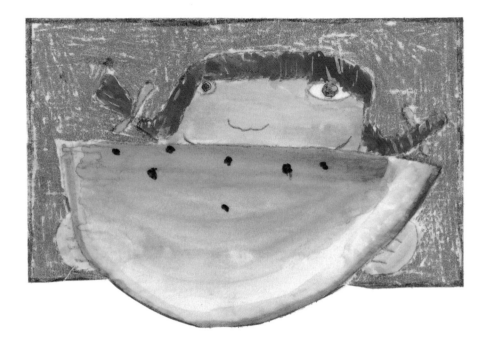

A SUMMERY

June: We seeded.
July: We weeded.
August: We eated.

THREE WORDS

Three words
Most cruel:
Back to school.

Fireflies

Fire
> fire
  fire-
> flies.
Igniting
> up
  the
> evening
>> skies.
Twilight
> flashlights
  phosphorescent.
Sky-light
> de-lights
  incandescent.
>> Lime-light
  night lights
for retiring.
> In-flight
>> taillights
AWE-inspiring.

CAMPFIRE

The campfire burns.
The marshmallows toast.
And now a story
About a ghost
Who roamed around
These woods at night,
A hideous horrible
Terrible sight.
Without a sound
And out of view
He'd sneak behind children.
There's one behind YOU!

SUMMER NIGHT

On this splendid summer night
Bullfrogs belch beneath moonlight.
While they're burping, chirping crickets
Quickly hop among the thickets.
As mosquitos buzz your ear,
Green cicadas you may hear.
Now's the time when one enjoys
All this splendid summer noise.

Pack up

Quick!
Before the summer's gone—
Pack a rosy-fingered dawn.
Pack a pond
Or ocean spray.
Pack them for a snow-packed day.